Basic Listening

Authentic recordings to develop listening micro-skills through graded tasks

John McDowell and Sandra Stevens

Edward Arnold
A division of Hodder & Stoughton
LONDON MELBOURNE AUCKLAND

© 1982 John McDowell and Sandra Stevens

First published in Great Britain 1982
Reprinted 1983 (twice), 1984, 1985, 1986, 1988, 1989

British Library Cataloguing in Publication Data

McDowell, John
  Basic listening.
  Student's book
  1. English language—Text-books for foreigners
  2. English language—Spoken language
  I. Title   II. Stevens, Sandra
  428.3'4   PE1128
  ISBN 0-7131-8069-2

Typeset in 10/11 pt Compugraphic Univers by Reproduction
Drawings Ltd
Printed and bound in Great Britain for Edward Arnold, the
educational, academic and medical publishing division of
Hodder and Stoughton Limited, 41 Bedford Square, London
WC1B 3DQ by The Bath Press, Avon and W. H. Ware

Exercise 1   Can you spell that, please?

Look at the pairs of surnames below. In each case the pronunciation of 'a' and 'b' is the same. On the tape you will hear six people spelling one name in each pair. Write down which one they spell, 'a' or 'b'.

1 a Bead
   b Bede
2 a Reid
   b Read
3 a Grey
   b Gray

4 a Leslie
   b Lesley
5 a Stewart
   b Stuart
6 a Stephens
   b Stevens

Exercise 2

1   Who's your doctor?
Sally and Peter are friends. Sally has just moved to the same area as Peter and she is asking him for some information about his doctor. Listen and write down the following details.

Name
Address
Tel. No.

2   Where's the restaurant?
Chris is asking a friend for some information about a restaurant. Listen and write down the following information.

Name of the restaurant
Address
Tel. No.

Exercise 3   Enrolling at a language school.

Read the registration form below. Then listen to the conversation between the school secretary and a new student and write down the missing information.

Name (Capitals)	(Mr/Ms)

Address

Age   Nationality

Dates of Desired Course:
from 14th JANUARY   to 31st MARCH
Intensive:
☐ Monday to Friday   9.15 – 4.45

Semi-Intensive:
Either
☐ Programme A
Monday, Wednesday, Friday   9.15 – 12.15
Tuesday and Thursday   1.45 – 4.45
Or
☐ Programme B
Tuesday and Thursday   9.15 – 12.15
Monday, Wednesday, Friday   1.45 – 4.45

Exercise 1 International Dialling Codes.

Read the list of towns and international dialling codes below. You will hear five different people telephoning the International Service to check the codes. While you listen, write a tick (√) if the code is right. If it is wrong, write the correct code number.

1 Belgrade, Yugoslavia 010 38 31
2 Sydney, Australia 010 61 2
3 Athens, Greece 010 381
4 Hamburg, Germany 010 59 50
5 Riyadh, Saudi Arabia 010 966 11

Exercise 2 Directory Enquiries.

Read carefully the names and addresses below. You will hear five different people telephoning Directory Enquiries to ask for a number. The names and addresses below are not in the same order as on the tape. First, identify which name and address you hear, then write down the telephone number.
   e.g. **6** f *925 0136*

a T. Snelling, 14a Melrose Road, CARDIFF.
b Philip Barnett, 21 Blenheim Crescent, GLASGOW.
c P. Winters, 93 Bodley Lane, PORTSMOUTH.
d Alec Lea, 1 Elm Road, BIRMINGHAM.
e K. Neale, 117 Cliff Lane, BRIGHTON.
f Sarah Hempson, 11 Clifford Road, GUILDFORD.

Exercise 3

1 A reverse-charge call.
Listen to this woman asking for a reverse-charge call to a number in Milton Keynes, a town north of London, and write down the following details.

Caller's number
Caller's name
Number calling

2 A person-to-person call.
Listen to this woman making a person-to-person call to someone in the United States and write down the following details.

The number she's calling
The person she's calling
Her name

Exercise 1   What do they do?

You will hear six people asking what other people do. Write down the jobs you hear.
   e.g. **7** *dentist*

Exercise 2   Here's a job for you.

On the tape, there are four conversations. In each one, a person is talking about an advertisement for a job. Copy the chart below and, while you listen, fill it in.

	Job	Salary	Hours
1			
2			
3			
4			

Exercise 3   What do I do?

Listen to these four people talking about their daily work routine, and write down what each person does.
   e.g. **5** *teacher*

Exercise 4   Where are they?

Look at the plan opposite. Listen to the six different people talking and decide where they are.
   e.g. **7** *hospital*

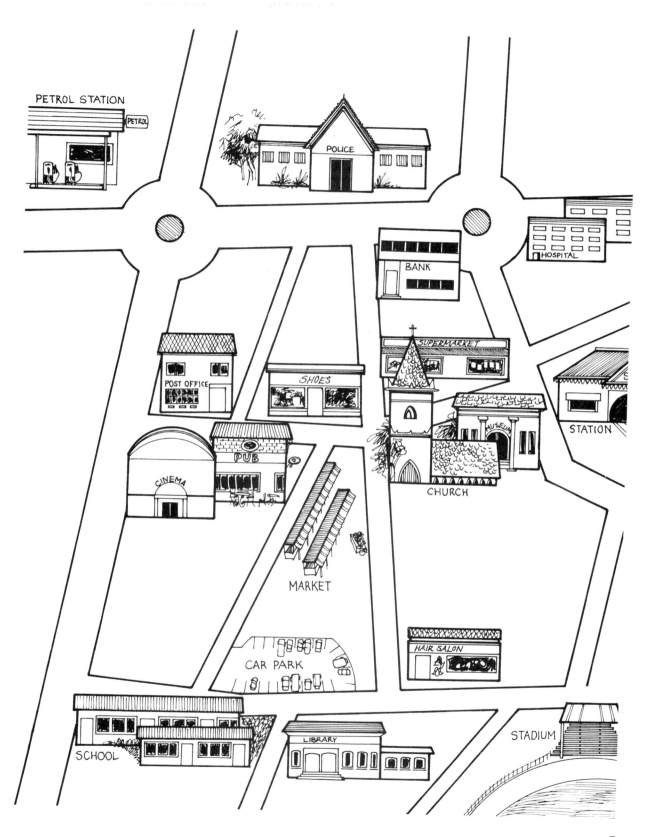

PETROL STATION

PETROL

POLICE

BANK

HOSPITAL

POST OFFICE

SHOES

SUPERMARKET

STATION

CINEMA

PUB

MUSEUM

CHURCH

MARKET

CAR PARK

HAIR SALON

SCHOOL

LIBRARY

STADIUM

Exercise 1   What's the time?

Listen to these people asking the time and write down the six different times you hear.
e.g. **7** *10.25*

Exercise 2   When are you open?

Listen to the people asking the opening hours of the three places shown below and write down the times you hear.

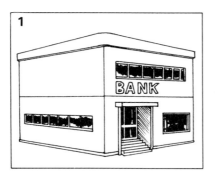

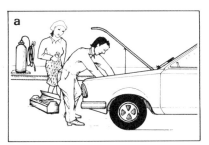

Exercise 3   When is it?

Look at the pictures above. You will hear people talking about when
five of the situations shown will take place. Match the conversations
with the correct picture and write down when they will be.

e.g. **6** *Picture h—next Tuesday, 4 o'clock*

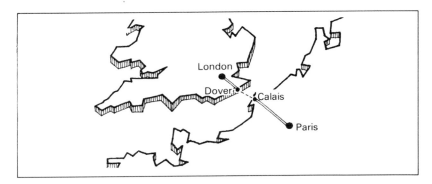

Exercise 4   How long did it take?

You will hear John telling Sally how long it took him to drive from
London to Paris by the route shown above. Listen and write down the
number of hours.

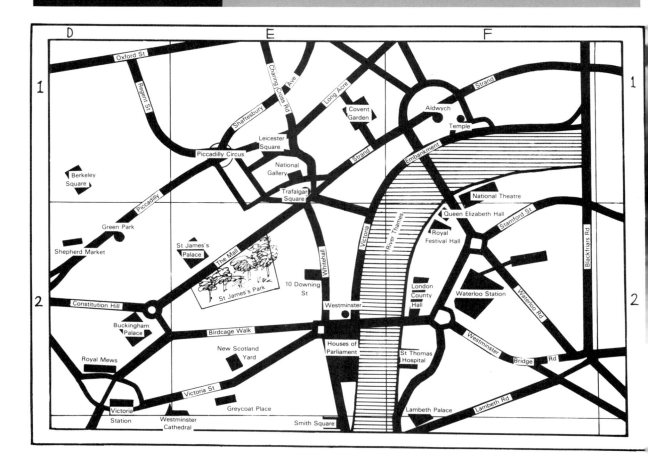

Exercise 1   Where is it?

Look at the map of an area of London. You will hear people looking for four different places. As you listen, find the places and write down which square they are in.

> *e.g.* **5** *Buckingham Palace D2*

1 Leicester Square   **3** Covent Garden
2 The Houses of Parliament   **4** Waterloo Station

Exercise 2   Where shall we meet?

You will hear four different conversations. In each one a person is arranging to meet a friend. Look at the map at the top of the next page. For each of the conversations, two people, a and b, are shown waiting in different places. Listen and decide which person is waiting in the correct place.

> *e.g.* **5** *a*

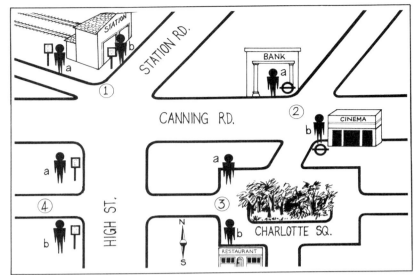

☻ **Underground Station**

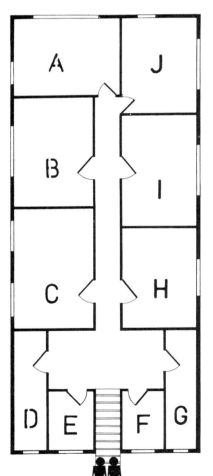

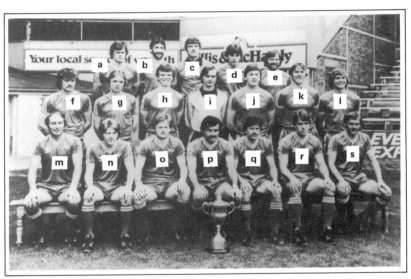

Exercise 3   Which one's Peter?

Look at the picture of the football team above. Listen and write down where the following people are.

e.g. David c

1 Peter   **2** Paul   **3** Tom

Exercise 4   Where's room 4?

Look at the plan of one floor of a school building. You will hear four people asking where different rooms are. Listen and match the four rooms mentioned with the corresponding letters. Note that the speakers are standing at the bottom of the stairs.

e.g. C classroom

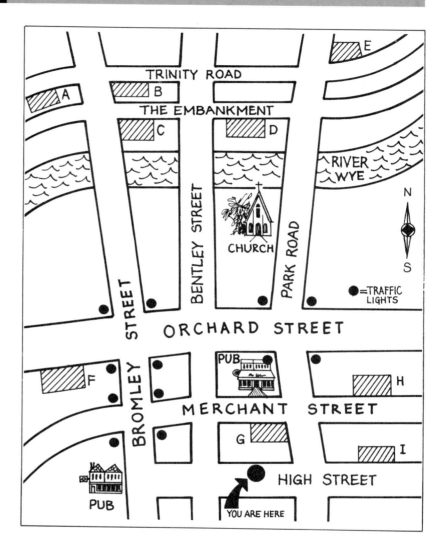

Exercise 1 Can you tell me the way, please?

Look at the map above. You will hear four people asking the way to four different places on the map. The places are marked with letters. Listen and write down the place each person is asking about and which letter it is on the map. Notice that the people are standing in High Street, at the spot marked 'YOU ARE HERE'.

e.g. Market I

Exercise 2   How do I get there?

You will hear three people telling you how to get to their homes.
Listen and make notes on what you hear.

1 Anne is telling you how to get to her house from the tube station.
2 Jane is telling you how to get to her house from the tube station.
3 Pat is telling you how to get to her house by car from Bedford
Square.

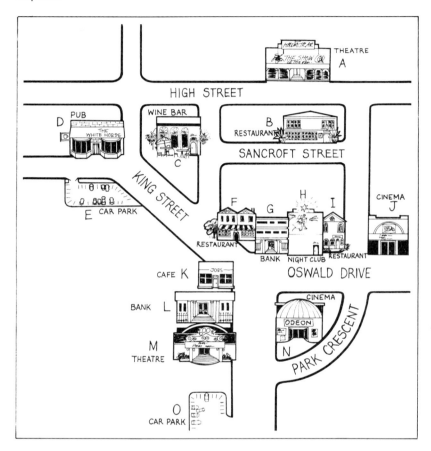

Exercise 3   What did you do last night?

Look carefully at the map of Northfields above. Listen to Robert
telling Gill what he did last night and where he went. Write down the
places he visited in the correct order.

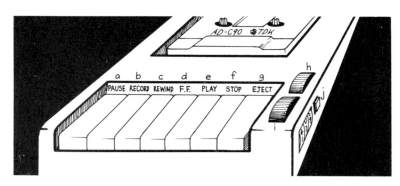

Exercise 1   Can you tell me how this machine works, please?

Look carefully at the cassette-recorder above and notice there is a letter next to each one of the buttons. Listen to Sue telling John how to use the machine and write down her instructions in the correct order, using the letters. There are seven instructions.

e.g. **8** *j*

Exercise 2   It works like this.

Look at the eight pictures below. You will hear six people, each one explaining how to use one of these machines. Write down the names of the machines in the order of the descriptions.

e.g. **7** *camera*

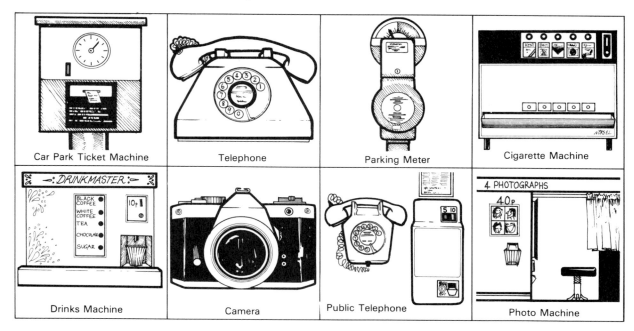

Exercise 1   How much is it?

Look at the articles and prices below. Listen to six people asking how much these things cost and match each article with the correct price.
   e.g. shoes £20.15

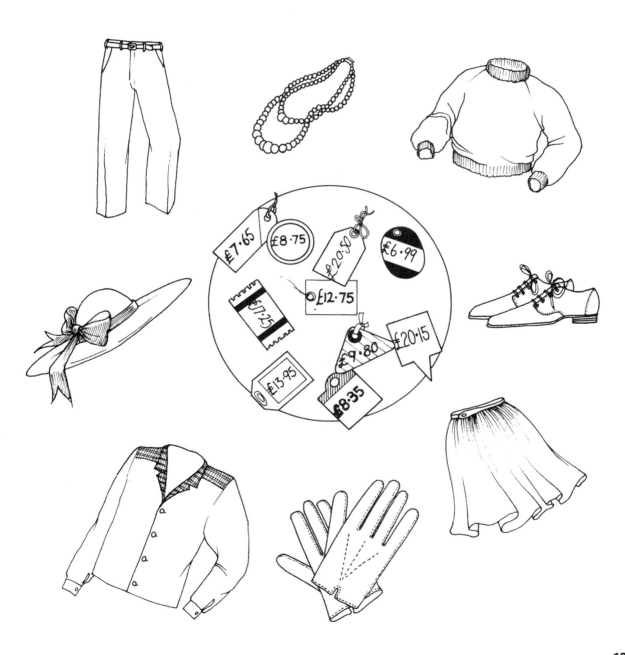

Exercise 2 That's £1.15 please.

Listen to these conversations at the cash desk in three different shops. First, write down the price of each item, check the total and then decide which is the correct sum of money to pay for each, a, b, c or d.

1 writing paper
birthday card
pen

Total

2 potatoes
biscuits
cheese
milk

Total

3 shampoo
soap
toothbrush

Total

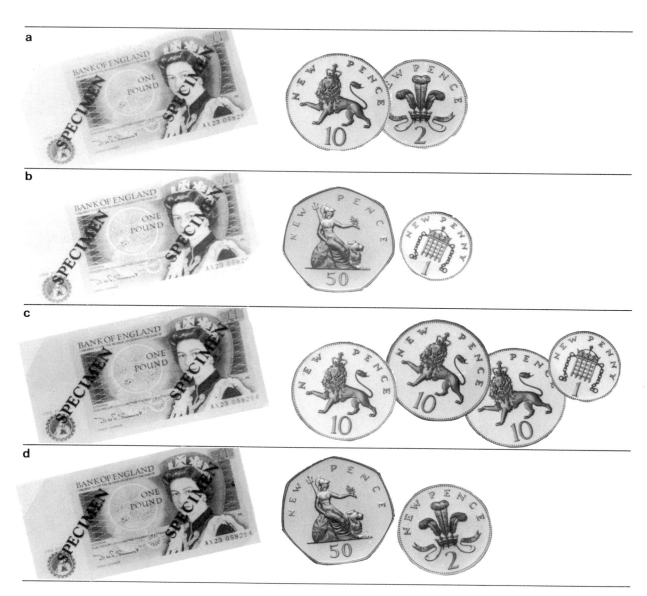

a

b

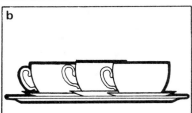

c

d

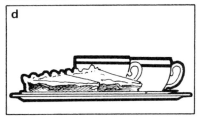

e

f

Exercise 3　Three coffees.

1 Look at the six trays of snacks on the left. Listen to the cashiers adding up five of the bills and match each bill with the correct tray.
  e.g. **6** *g*

2 Below is the menu of the same snack bar as in part 1. Read the menu and look at the prices. You will hear the same tape again. This time add up the bill for each tray. If the total on the tape is correct, write a tick (√). If it is wrong, write the correct total.

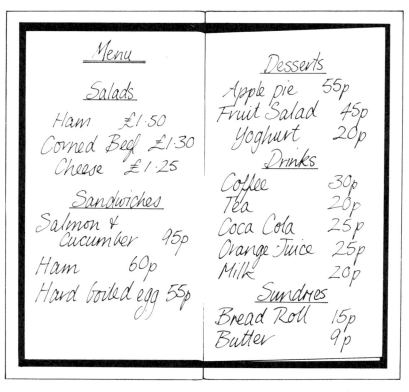

Menu

Salads

Ham　　　£1·50
Corned Beef　£1·30
Cheese　　£1·25

Sandwiches

Salmon &
　Cucumber　95p
Ham　　60p
Hard boiled egg 55p

Desserts

Apple pie　55p
Fruit Salad　45p
Yoghurt　20p

Drinks

Coffee　　30p
Tea　　　20p
Coca Cola　25p
Orange Juice　25p
Milk　　20p

Sundries

Bread Roll　15p
Butter　　9p

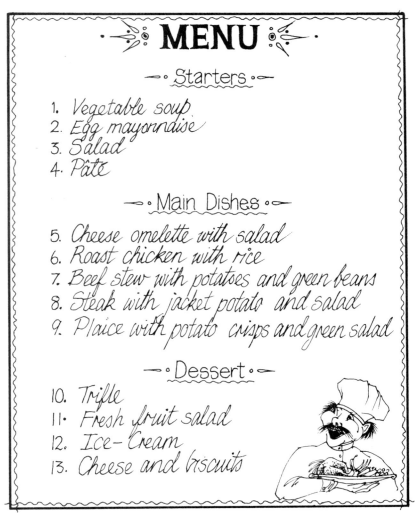

⋅≫⋅ MENU ⋅≪⋅

⋅ Starters ⋅

1. Vegetable soup
2. Egg mayonnaise
3. Salad
4. Pâté

⋅ Main Dishes ⋅

5. Cheese omelette with salad
6. Roast chicken with rice
7. Beef stew with potatoes and green beans
8. Steak with jacket potato and salad
9. Plaice with potato crisps and green salad

⋅ Dessert ⋅

10. Trifle
11. Fresh fruit salad
12. Ice-Cream
13. Cheese and biscuits

Exercise 1   What would you like?

Look at the menu above. Listen to the people ordering a meal and write down their order. Write only the number for each dish.
e.g. 1 × No. 4

Exercise 2   Do you want anything?

Listen to Sandra and John ordering a snack lunch. Write down what they ask for.

Sandra
John

Exercise 3 Is there anything you can't eat?

Three people are telling their landladies what they can't eat. Listen and write down the food they say.

1 Margo   **2** Mr Rice   **3** Mick

Exercise 4 How do you make it?

Listen to Margaret and Mike telling you how they cook or make two dishes and write down the ingredients.

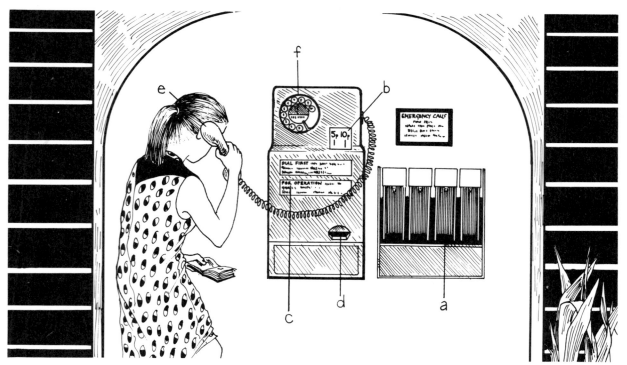

Exercise 1   How does it work?

Look carefully at the public telephone above and notice the position of the letters. Listen to this woman explaining how to use it and write down her instructions in the correct order, using the letters.

e.g. **7** *g*

Exercise 2   What's it about?

You will hear only one side of six conversations. Write down what each conversation is about.

Sarah,
Tim phoned—
Please meet him at
the station at
8.30.
Peter

Exercise 3 Can you take a message?

Read the telephone message above. You will hear three conversations where a person is leaving a message. Write down the three messages.

Exercise 1 What does she look like?

Look at the five sketches below and notice that there is a letter next to each one. You will hear descriptions of three of the women. Identify which ones are being described.

 e.g. **4** *d*

a

b

c

d

e

Exercise 2 What did he look like?

Look at the form below. It contains the details of a suspect in a bank robbery. You will hear three people describing men they saw near the bank at the time of the robbery.

1 Listen and make notes like the ones below.
2 Compare your notes with those of the man below and decide which of your descriptions corresponds with that of the suspect.

Height: 6' 1"
Hair: brown
Eyes: brown
Clothes: jeans, sweater
Other details: beard, thin

Exercise 3 Has anyone seen this person?

On the tape you will hear two announcements about missing persons. Listen and take notes.

Exercise 1   Which one is it?

Look at the four pictures below. Listen to the tape and decide which two are being described.

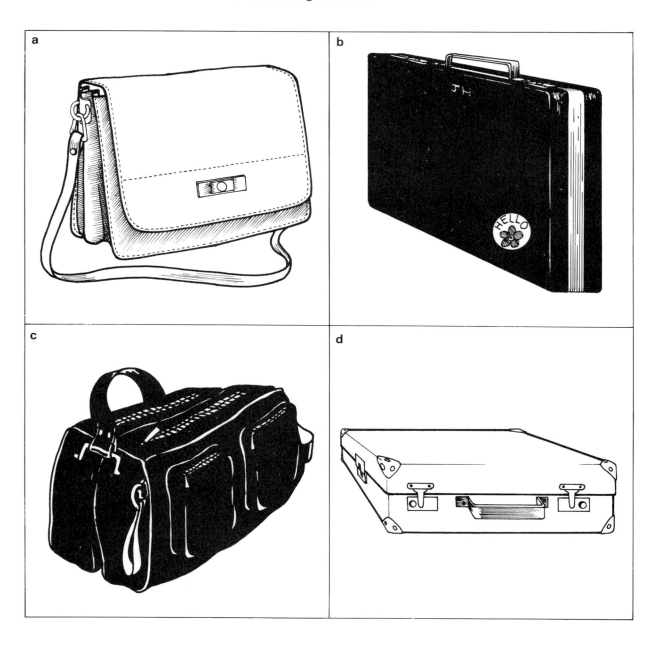

Exercise 2 Could you describe it to me, please?

Listen to these three people describing some things they have lost. While you listen, take notes.

Exercise 3 A guessing game.

In these five conversations one person has thought of an object and the other person is asking questions to find out what it is. Can you guess what the object is?

Exercise 1   We've got a house for you.

Look at the four advertisements of houses for sale below. You will hear an estate agent offering three of the houses to three different clients. Match each client with the house offered.

1 Jones family   **2** Herbert family   **3** Wilson family

a

For Sale

Small comfortable flat
near shops and station.
1 bed., 1 din/sit. room,
kit., bathroom and toilet.
Ground floor.

b

For Sale

Modern semi-detached house.
Front and back garden.
Nr town centre. 3 beds.,
sit. rm/din. rm., kit.,
bthrm.

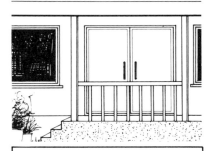

c

For Sale

Comfortable flat near park.
Very modern. 2 beds.,
din. room, kit., bthrm.,
2 toilets, small garden.

d

For Sale

Luxury house – extensive
garden. Double garage – full
central heating. 6 beds.,
large sit. room, large din.
rm., 2 fitted kitchens.

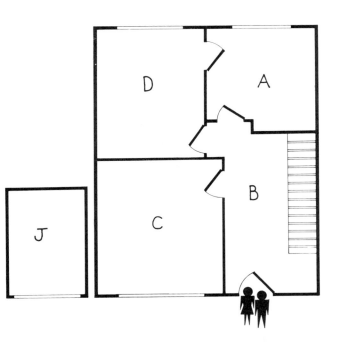

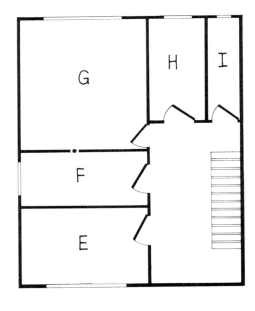

Exercise 2 This is the house.

Look at the house plan above. A man from the estate agent's is showing a client, Mrs Walker, round the house. Listen and match the names of the different rooms with their corresponding letters.

e.g. J = garage

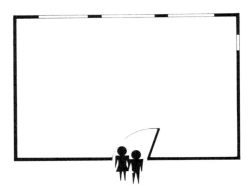

Exercise 3 Where shall I put it?

Look at the plan of the room above. You will hear two people discussing where to put the furniture. Copy the plan and, as you listen, mark in the position of the different pieces of furniture. Notice that the people are standing at the door, looking into the room as they talk.

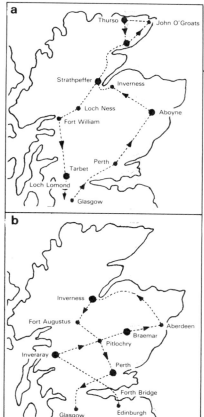

Exercise 1   Choose your holiday.

Listen to the travel agent describing three holiday tours and match them with the correct route maps shown below.

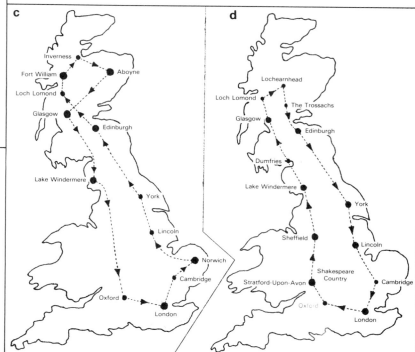

Exercise 2   I'd like a room, please.

Copy the hotel registration form below. Listen to the man telephoning the hotel to book a room, and fill in the form.

Royal Hotel 17 Princess Gardens
Tel. 247-634

Name

Date of arrival

Length of stay

Room (double/single)

Time of arrival

Exercise 3 Having a lovely time.

Look at these three holiday postcards. They were written by different people. You will hear two of the people talking about their holiday. Listen and match them with the postcards they wrote.

a

NOVA LVX

Tuesday

Five days just isn't long enough here. The city is even more beautiful than you said. I've spent hours just wandering round galleries and museums. Even just sitting out in the street is a pleasure. I've taken tons of photos.

Take care, love

Roger

86

b

Having a wonderful time here, just living on the golf course. The flight out was good, and we've settled into a beautiful house near the beach. You'd love it. See you when we get back.

Fred.

c

Tuesday.

Spent 5 days driving down here — a bit awful but now we're relaxing on the beach before going down south and getting into some serious sightseeing!!

Passed by Chartres Cathedral on the way — remember?

Simon

COMERCIAL ESCUDO DE ORO, S.A.
Pajaudarias 26
Reproducción prohibida

27

LONDON—HAMBURG

DEPART London, Heathrow Airport. BA flights: Terminal 1 (Minimum check-in time at pier gate 20 mins)
                         Other flights: Terminal 2 (Minimum check-in time 30 mins)
ARRIVE Hamburg, Fuhlsbüttel Airport

	Frequency	Aircraft Dep	Arr	Via	Transfer Times	Flight	Aircraft	Class & Catering	
a	Daily	0900	1125(y)	non-stop		BA734	TRD	FY	✖
b	Daily to 27 Sep	1055	1320	non-stop		LH041	72⁷ (a)	FY	⊗
c	Daily from 28 Sep	1155	1320	non-stop		LH041	727 (a)	FY	⊗
d	Daily	1525	1750(y)	non-stop		BA736	TRD	FY	ⵖ
e	Daily to 27 Sep	1930	2155	non-stop		LH045	AB3	FY	✖
f	Daily from 28 Sep	2030	2155	non-stop		LH045	AB3	FY	✖

Exercise 1

1   I want to fly to Hamburg.

Look at the air timetable above. You will hear a man buying a ticket to Hamburg. Which flight is he going to travel on?

NEWCASTLE

	a	b	c	d	e
King's Cross	10^{05}	12^{20}	13^{35}	19^{25}	19^{53}
Newcastle	14^{30}	16^{35}	18^{05}	23^{40}	00^{20}

2   Can you tell me the times of the trains to Newcastle?

Look at the train timetable above. You will hear someone asking about trains to Newcastle. Which train is he going to travel on?

Exercise 2 Would passengers please...?

Look at the departures board below. You will hear three announcements. Listen and decide which flight each announcement refers to. Then write down where the passengers should go.

e.g. **4** f *check-in*

	FLIGHT	DESTINATION
a	AIR NEW ZEALAND - 249	AUCKLAND..
b	IBERIA - 420	MADRID...
c	VARIG - 397	SAO PAULO..
d	ALITALIA - 242	ROME ...
e	BRITISH AIRWAYS - 265	ROTTERDAM..

Exercise 3 May I have your attention, please?

Listen to the five travel announcements and match them with the corresponding picture below.